Healing After Betrayal

JUST A MINUTE MEDITATIONS

Healing After Betrayal

BY KATHRYN J. HERMES, FSP

Pauline
BOOKS & MEDIA
Boston

Library of Congress Control Number: 2025933448

ISBN 10: 0-8198-3476-9

ISBN 13: 978-0-8198-3476-8

Cover design by Tisa Muico

Published by Pauline Books & Media, 50 Saint Pauls Avenue, Boston, MA 02130-3491

Printed in the USA

www.pauline.org

Pauline Books & Media is the publishing house of the Daughters of St. Paul, an international congregation of women religious serving the Church with the communications media.

1 2 3 4 5 6 7 8 9 30 29 28 27 26 25

Contents

Introduction 1

1. Lord, This Is My Honest Prayer 5

2. I Choose Healing Today 7

3. I Hear You Call My Name 9

4. Show Me, Lord, How You Have Loved Me 11

5. Lord, I Give You What Hurts 13

6. Come, Jesus, and Find Me 15

7. You Heal Me Gradually 17

8. Lord, You Make Good Things Happen for Me 19

9. Give Me New Memories 21

10. Lord, You Still Have a Dream for My Future 23

11. I Plunge into Your Grace 25

12. Your Vision for Me Is Far from Over 27

13. You Are the God Who Sees Me 29

14. You Make Me Feel Safe and Loved 31

15. You Show Me the Precious Value of My Life 33

16. You Touch Every Human Heart 35

17. You've Called Me for a Purpose 37
18. The Lord Will Never Leave Me 39
19. Jesus, Show Me the Next Step 41
20. I Am Ready, O God 43
21. Jesus, You Help Me Move On 45
22. Jesus, You Have Changed the Course of My Life 47
23. Lord, I Desire Everything You Wish for Me Now 49
24. Jesus, Help Me to Love Bravely 51
25. Open My Heart to Love Again 53
26. I Renounce the Lies I Have Believed 55
27. Lord, You Are Making All Things New 57
28. You Show Me a Better Way 59
29. I'm Beginning to See That You Are Faithful 61
30. How Can I Thank You? 63
Prayers 65
    Psalm 18 65
    Enter My Life 67
    A Prayer to Believe in Love 67
    Heal Me, Lord 69
    Sub Tuum Praesidium 69
    Prayer for the Healing of Memories 70
    Heart of Love 71

Introduction

How did I not see this coming? Have you ever thought this when a situation didn't turn out the way you expected because someone you trusted let you down?

Recall a time when you felt you could trust others without second guessing. A time before a loved one didn't take responsibility for inexcusable behavior, or someone didn't follow through on a promise, or a close relationship began to fray because of the other's addictive behaviors or infidelity, or you were criticized in front of others, or a friend spoke harshly about you behind your back.

Whether the situation is serious or less so, betrayal hurts. Betrayal wounds. It is hard to recover from the cruel disappointment we feel when someone we love and trust turns out to be on a different page altogether. We question ourselves, or even kick ourselves for being so blind, so utterly trusting. Where did we go wrong?

Trust can be broken through a misunderstanding, an inadvertent remark, a decision made under duress that had a negative impact on us. Betrayals can cut deeply.

When a spouse walks out, every anniversary is a reminder of the rejection and loss. The abuse of someone we trusted can be so devastating we may not recover for years. When no one sees the pain we're suffering because of a wrong that has been done to us, our loneliness can be excruciating.

Regardless of the strong faith we thought we had, when someone disappoints us, it stings. We want to end this bruising of our heart. We want things to go back to the way they were. But sooner or later we must accept that our life will never be the same. New horizons will open up, but it's unlikely we will recover what has been lost.

The good news is this: the Word of God points us toward realities that lie deeper than we can see with the naked eye. God's holy Word gives us a place to go when our soul needs to breathe and our heart needs to heal. In praying with the Word of God we discover something deeper than anything we have suffered and greater than all we have lost. In prayer we sense that God loves us personally and intimately. In the Scriptures we come to know that Jesus, who himself suffered betrayal and disappointment, calls us his friends and opens to us the depths of his very heart. In story, parable, and teaching,

Jesus speaks tenderly to us of realities that lift us out of our sorrow.

View the meditations in this book as the whispers from a friend who understands the questions you are asking. These short reflections on God's Word are like a hand reaching out to you from someone who knows that healing is not neat and tidy, that it's a daily battle. These scriptural words from the God who created you, the Good Shepherd, the Crucified and Risen One, are promises that, as you walk through difficult days, you will receive the help you need.

Friend, this is deep soul work. As you pray these pages you might find it helpful to follow the pattern suggested below. This pattern may be new to you; it might even feel upside down, counterintuitive for someone who is still processing the unfairness of life and dealing with too many unknowns. However, this new rhythm may be just what you need to find your anchor.

1. Begin with the future by praying: *I thank you, God, for holding all my tomorrows. I do not know what will happen to me, but I know that you are already there preparing the way.*
2. Carry only today's grace. Don't bring into your prayer all that happened in the past or your

fears of the future. Read each meditation focusing on the gift God is giving you today.

3. Choose to sit in the quietness. Let each meditation settle within you softly, gently, as it teaches you something about God, about yourself, and about who God created you to be.
4. Open your hands to God. This isn't an ending, no matter what has ruptured the sense of continuity in your life. God sees. God knows. God listens to you. After this pause along the way, God will show you where and how to begin trusting again.
5. End with faith. Release back to God whatever you are anxious or uncertain about. Thank him for the Scripture you have prayed with and turn it into your personal Credo. Start with "I believe . . ." Insert your own name or situation where appropriate. And end with "I believe."

1

Lord, This Is My Honest Prayer

It is not enemies who taunt me—
I could bear that;
it is not adversaries who deal insolently with me—
I could hide from them.
But it is you, my equal,
my companion, my familiar friend. . . .
Cast your burden on the LORD,
and he will sustain you.

PSALM 55:12–13, 22

These words of King David were likely penned when rebellion had broken out against him. His own son Absalom had stolen the hearts of the men of Israel. Even his trusted counselor, Ahithophel, had abandoned him and supported the attempt to usurp the throne from David. Violence, strife, and destruction were rampant in Jerusalem as the king fled.

David was no stranger to betrayal. He had been betrayed by King Saul. He himself had betrayed Uriah after having relations with Uriah's wife: to hide his offense the king had arranged for the good soldier to be killed in battle. And now his trusted counselor and his own son had betrayed him.

In this fallen world, we too will suffer the sting of betrayal, infidelity, and injustice at the hands of people we thought were on our side. So what does David show us in this psalm? When your life is upended by another's infidelity, abuse, or dishonesty, bring your anguish and anger to God in honest prayer and trust him to sustain you.

O God, I need your help, for I am alone and no one else knows what I am going through.

2

I Choose Healing Today

> I command you: be strong and steadfast! Do not fear nor be dismayed, for the LORD, your God, is with you wherever you go.
>
> Joshua 1:9 NABRE

When you've been betrayed—deceived, tricked, double-crossed, stabbed in the back—anger, guilt, depression, anxiety, self-hatred, and a host of other issues can take over your life. Months and years may be stolen from you and your loved ones as you try to recover what you've lost: the time, the money, the relationship, the self-worth, the courage to get on with life.

It takes courage to journey beyond the place, the day, the relationship in which your expectations and trust were taken from you. It takes courage to dare to hope today. It takes courage to take the first of many significant steps. The most important thing is to start and to keep walking, to remember that each step—whether it seems large or small, whether it seems to be taking you forward or backward—is part of the dynamic process of healing that will continue through the span of your life. Remember, small detours are part of the whole picture.

Healing is all about giving yourself a chance *today*.

Jesus, you never leave me alone. I take courage in your promise and choose healing today.

3

I Hear You Call My Name

"Come to me, all you that are weary and are carrying heavy burdens, and I will give you rest."

Matthew 11:28

It could take years to realize how much emotional, psychological, or spiritual damage we've lived with after betrayal by someone we trusted. We may be unaware of how our relationships with God and others are colored or crippled by guilt, fear, or shame. Even though our lives might appear to be flourishing, exhaustion and stress may weigh us down as we feel unsupported, ignored, or inadequate in the face of unresolved issues that we may not entirely understand.

Does any of this ring a bell? What is it like to carry this alone?

At this moment, Jesus wants to draw near to you. Hear him addressing you by name and saying: I see the weight of the burden you're carrying. I hear you crying out for relief. Come to me. I will support you as you reclaim your life. I will alleviate your exhaustion and give you rest as you face the issues you can no longer ignore. Whatever you are experiencing, be gentle with yourself. We will journey together. You are not alone, and you never were.

Lord, I'm afraid to lay down my burden. It's everything that I know. But if you stay beside me, I won't be anxious about the journey ahead.

4

Show Me, Lord, How You Have Loved Me

> With age-old love I have loved you;
>   so I have kept my mercy toward you.
> Again I will build you, and you shall stay built. . . .
> You shall again plant vineyards
>   on the mountains of Samaria;
>   those who plant them shall enjoy their fruits.
>
> JEREMIAH 31:3–5 NABRE

As you read this passage, relax. In whatever way is possible during these hard times, open your heart to the "age-old" and "forever" love of the Lord, a love that had no beginning and which at this moment embraces you in your sorrow.

There may be tears, or there may be no tears. There may be memories, or there may be no memories. There may be seething anger, confusion, or loss. Or there may be numbness. For healing, each of us begins from our own place. It's important to recognize that healing does not begin with the wound. The foundation of your life is much deeper. It extends back in your life-story to before your birth. It is a love story. The true foundation of your life is God's love for you, a love that was there before the world was created.

In this passage from Jeremiah, God reminds us that he can and will rebuild the one he loves.

Ask the Lord to show you what you need to know about his next step for your healing.

God of love, you will rebuild what is broken, mend what is torn, find what is lost, hold what is hurting.

5

Lord, I Give You What Hurts

He has cast me into the mire,
    and I have become like dust and ashes.
I cry to you and you do not answer me;
    I stand, and you merely look at me. . . .
I go about in sunless gloom;
    I stand up in the assembly and cry for help. . . .
My lyre is turned to mourning.

Job 30:19–20, 28, 31

These complaints from the heart of Job ring true for many who've been duped or misled by a person or group they thought was trustworthy. It is important to protest, to grieve, to lament this way. No matter what is in your heart, God wants to hear from you.

This is a way to begin clearing your heart:

Imagine yourself seated at a table with Jesus beside you. Ask yourself, "What is my deepest feeling about what happened?" When you are ready, in your inspired imagination, take this feeling in your hands and place it on the table. Say to yourself, "Yes, that feeling is mine, but it isn't all my feelings." Then hand this feeling to Jesus. Give him your insecurity at feeling unloved or unwanted, your shame at feeling worthless, the trepidation that you might never regain what you have lost, your sense of being abandoned, or your fear that nothing can get better.

Notice that when Jesus takes everything that you hand over to him, he holds it all gently.

Take a deep breath. Rest at this point.

Dear Jesus, the wounds I have received have led me to isolate myself from others and even to hide from you. Today I choose to hand over all this to you.

6

Come, Jesus, and Find Me

> The other disciples told [Thomas], "We have seen the Lord." But he said to them, "Unless I see the mark of the nails in his hands, and put my finger in the mark of the nails and my hand in his side, I will not believe."
>
> John 20:25

Before the trauma that the apostles experienced with the Death of Christ, Thomas' heart would have trusted the other disciples' declaration that they had seen the Lord. But now, after all that had happened, Thomas stated firmly, "I will not believe."

The actions of someone who has hurt you do not define you. Nevertheless, betrayal in your life may be one of those "before and after" experiences. You may want to be the trusting, open person you once were. But now you're not—you can't be. You've seen too much. Others can offer comforting or well-intentioned words, but your heart may not understand, at least for a while.

Jesus understood what Thomas needed. When he appeared next, he invited Thomas to touch his wounds.

When the spiritual words of others fall flat, Jesus understands. He knows when you don't need words; you need him. You need to engage with Jesus, directly, gradually, coming closer and closer to him. By coming to find Thomas and bringing him into contact with his own most sacred wounds, Jesus helped Thomas to again find his place in the community of disciples.

Jesus, when I feel like I'll never find myself again or know you the way I knew you before, please come and find me.

7

You Heal Me Gradually

> He took the blind man by the hand and led him out of the village; and when he had put saliva on his eyes and laid his hands on him, he asked him, "Can you see anything?" And the man looked up and said, "I can see people, but they look like trees, walking." Then Jesus laid his hands on his eyes again; and he looked intently and his sight was restored, and he saw everything clearly.
>
> Mark 8:23–25

The healing stories of Jesus affirm for us the beauty of God's creation. Though a person may be blind, deaf, or suffering with leprosy or other illness, we see from Jesus' care that this person is precious in God's sight. As Jesus heals, he lifts up and restores each person to his or her full beauty.

In the narrative above, healing takes place in two stages. In your own process of restoration, recovery of wholeness may take place in several stages. First comes the crossing through treacherous and sometimes churning waters of dealing with what has happened. After that you may feel better, but exhausted and alone. In subsequent stages you may have to deal with trust issues or decide how you will seek justice. Remember, you are brought to wholeness gradually. Healing is a lifelong journey.

Jesus, when I feel frustrated with myself because I haven't finished the work of healing, help me to appreciate all the stages through which I have passed on the way to peace.

8

Lord, You Make Good Things Happen for Me

> O afflicted one, storm-battered and unconsoled,
>   I lay your pavements in carnelians,
>   your foundations in sapphires;
> I will make your battlements of rubies,
>   your gates of jewels,
>   and all your walls of precious stones.
>
> Isaiah 54:11–12 NABRE

This promise of God to his afflicted people is a passage I sit with when I find myself overwhelmed by troubles. Sometimes it's with clenched teeth, willing myself to believe. At other times I have a softened heart, as I trustingly yield to a love wiser than my own.

The beauty of this promise is that it helps us reframe our perspective. It gives us some solid ground to stand on when our emotions and reactions are swirling within us, creating their own narrative. This promise tells us that God sees us. God hears us. And God is doing something about what we're suffering.

When you are suffering from another's actions that betrayed your trust, this passage shows that God is gazing kindly at *you*. Despite all you have been through, he says, I will make *you* beautiful, strong, and precious. *I, myself*, will do this.

Let the jewels that are listed in this passage be placeholders for the gifts that God sees you need. In prayer ask God to show you what he is already bringing about for you.

I thought, O Lord, that there was nothing left for me. But you make good things happen for me. Your love never ends.

9

Give Me New Memories

For as the heavens are high above the earth,
so great is his steadfast love toward those
who fear him. . . .
As a father has compassion for his children,
so the LORD has compassion for those who fear him.
For he knows how we were made;
he remembers that we are dust.

PSALM 103.11, 13–14

When others are out to hurt us, when they show up for everyone else but us, when no one sees our pain or confusion, the unfairness of it all can make us feel isolated and alone. Questioning whether God really cares, we might find it difficult to believe that his love is steadfast and trustworthy, that he will have compassion on us in our misery. We may even feel guilt for wanting to give up on God altogether.

Ask the Holy Spirit to help you meet God's compassion right in the midst of your pain. Lift up a memory related in some way to the hurt you have received. As the memory begins to play out like a movie, gently hit "pause." As you hold this memory, ask Jesus to show you where he was at that moment, or to show you where he is right now. Let the memory of the hurt from the betrayal fade away as Jesus gives you a new memory of the deeper reality of the way God cradles you in his arms.

Jesus, what do you want me to know about the pain I've been through? I will wait upon your word.

10

Lord, You Still Have a Dream for My Future

Then the LORD will guide you always
    and satisfy your thirst in parched places,
    will give strength to your bones
And you shall be like a watered garden,
    like a flowing spring whose waters never fail.

ISAIAH 58:11 NABRE

The shock of promises broken and trust betrayed, of relationship breakups and breakdowns, is deeply hurtful. You thought you could trust someone and now you're scared. You thought the future was secure, and you feel burned instead. You want to believe that someone loves you, but your gut tells you not to risk it. At these times the scattered ruins of your world seem no more than a pile of discarded stones. You may fear that the shards of your experience will never fit together again.

But God is inviting you to build your identity upon surer things. Betrayals alter your life. They bring you to turn a corner, find a new path, explore other horizons. They make you build a more stable foundation. Your heart has been fashioned for a trust that is eternal. Place your hope in the God whose love is *always*, in the Lord who will transform the stones of your disappointment into a garden that he himself waters from a never-failing spring.

O Lord, I collapse into your arms. You have designs for my life, a dream for my future. Give me strength, satisfy my thirst, and guide me always. Help me believe that you are leading me.

11

I Plunge into Your Grace

Our steps are made firm by the LORD,
    when he delights in our way;
though we stumble, we shall not fall headlong,
    for the LORD holds us by the hand. . . .
The LORD helps them and rescues them;
    he rescues them from the wicked, and saves them,
    because they take refuge in him.

PSALM 37:23–24, 40

Psalm 37 speaks of our steps being made firm even as we stumble, an image of the faith and resilience that the Lord gives us even as betrayal throws us headlong to the ground.

How do we find the firmness of this faith and the flexibility of this resilience?

It's impossible to control life altogether, to eliminate risk, avoid injustice, or ignore the pain of what you endure. Yet even when engulfed by a storm of grief, you needn't be drowned. You can find your way through it. You can plunge all the way to the bottom of it because Jesus is with you, and as the psalmist says: "the Lord holds us by the hand." In the deepest part of your sorrow, you will discover that you are still alive and there is hope. You're more resilient than you realized.

When you dive below the raging feelings, that very hurt can lead to amazing discoveries about yourself and about God. Strength you never recognized can thrive in adversity. The very suffering has become an invitation to plunge into God's grace.

When life gives me more than I can handle, Lord, help me and rescue me.

12
Your Vision for Me Is Far from Over

> For we are his handiwork, created in Christ Jesus for the good works that God has prepared in advance, that we should live in them.
>
> Ephesians 2:10 NABRE

As you process the pain of an unfair situation, disappointment can turn into sour bitterness. Maybe the pain has burned away, but your bruised heart is left feeling empty and deflated. The last thing you feel like is a magnificent work of art!

Yet the beauty, goodness, and truth of your life are not gifts of God that can be definitively broken and defaced by the actions of another. You may not be able to recapture who you were before experiencing the hurt, and that is all to the good. One day you must even drop any image of yourself as defined by wounds from the one who stole your trust. As you find fresh hope, meaning, and purpose in your life, you will be surprised that your relationship with God will take on new colors, shapes, and textures. One day it will become clear that God's vision for you is far from over—that in his creative process nothing has been lost.

Jesus, show me who I am. You alone truly know me. Show me who you are. My heart yearns for you.

13

You Are the God Who Sees Me

> The LORD's angel found her by a spring in the wilderness, the spring on the road to Shur, and he asked, "Hagar, maid of Sarai, where have you come from and where are you going?" She answered, "I am running away from my mistress, Sarai." . . .
>
> To the LORD who spoke to her she gave a name, saying, "You are God who sees me."
>
> Genesis 16:7–8, 13 NABRE

There are many beautiful names of God in Scripture. This is the name that Hagar gives to the Lord, who finds her when she is in distress: "You are God who sees me." The God who sees us is the one who counts our every tear, who knows everything about us, who never closes his eyes or misses a detail of what is happening in our lives.

When you don't feel God near, or if you think friendship with God is beyond your reach, ask yourself,

"What really stands between me and knowing God's strong love and enduring friendship?" In the passage above, notice it is the Lord who approaches Hagar first. She then tells him about her situation. She listens to his direction and then she addresses him by name.

The Lord is attending to you right now. He knows everything that is in your heart. Speak to him any way you know how. Then call God by this beautiful name: "You are God who sees me here and now."

When I feel I am lost, O Lord, you see me. I am never alone.

14

You Make Me Feel Safe and Loved

> "I am the good shepherd. The good shepherd lays down his life for the sheep."
>
> John 10:11

Jesus is Redeemer, Savior, Shepherd, Healer. The Son of God took on our humanity, choosing to embrace our vulnerable, fragile, and often tenuous earthly existence as his own. He did not come with overpowering demands or force us to bend to his desires. He came as a baby, poor, one of us. He knows from the inside out how we are made, what we feel, how we suffer, and also what frees us, draws us, makes us feel safe and loved.

These are the characteristics of a shepherd who lives—and is willing to die—for the life and well-being of those entrusted to his care. For those of us who have been betrayed through manipulation, deceit, and evil, Jesus is a Shepherd whom we can allow to draw near to us, for he will not use us or hurt us.

Yet, Jesus knows that to trust him after all you've been through may be a challenge. As the best of shepherds, he extends his hand to you and waits patiently until you are ready to reach out and place your own hand in his. See him looking into your eyes right now, asking quietly, "Do you trust me?"

Jesus, what has happened to me cannot be undone. Draw me to your side, feed me with your Body and Blood, walk with me through every moment of life, and welcome me one day into the unending embrace of your Father, where I will make my home with you forever.

15

You Show Me the Precious Value of My Life

> One of his disciples, the one whom Jesus loved, was reclining at Jesus' side. . . . He leaned back against Jesus' chest.
>
> John 13:23, 25 NABRE

The heartbeat of Jesus, the heartbeat of God. On that dark night when he would be arrested, mocked, and imprisoned, Jesus let his beloved disciple rest his head on his heart.

Jesus wants *you* to rest *your* head on his most Sacred Heart, ever pulsing with love. Why? Because he wants you to know the truth of his love for you and the precious value of your life.

In your inspired imagination, draw near to Jesus on this last night before he died for love of you. It may not be easy for you to approach Jesus so closely. Give yourself time; honor your feelings. Perhaps reach out to hold the edge of his garment. Watch his face while maintaining some distance. Then lay your head on his shoulder. Soak in this sense of nearness to your God. When you are ready, rest your head on Jesus' heart.

Regardless of the way you were wounded, your spiritual life and your relationship with God have surely been deeply affected, for being able to believe in love is at the foundation of all spiritual growth. Ultimately, no words will convince you of God's love—only the beating of Jesus' most Sacred Heart.

Jesus, I trust in you.

16

You Touch Every Human Heart

In the beginning was the Word, and the Word was with God, and the Word was God. He was in the beginning with God. All things came into being through him, and without him not one thing came into being. . . . And the Word became flesh and lived among us, and we have seen his glory, the glory as of a father's only son, full of grace and truth.

John 1:1–3, 14

Christ came into the darkness of a fallen world. The Word was made flesh. God took on our humanity, uniting himself to each person who has ever lived and will ever live.

The infinite God walked among us in Galilee at a specific time in history, but his Life, Death, and Resurrection are of cosmic significance. They touch every human life. They touch your life. As Saint Paul says, "In him we have redemption through his blood, the forgiveness of our trespasses, according to the riches of his grace that he lavished on us" (Ephesians 1:7–8).

Christ continues to be mysteriously but genuinely present and incarnate in the world through the Church. He works powerfully in your life in the Eucharist and in the Sacrament of Reconciliation. And every day, at every hour, Jesus is at work behind the scenes more than you could ever imagine—for when the Word became flesh he united himself to you.

Jesus, help me hear you speaking to my heart.

17

You've Called Me for a Purpose

> We know that all things work for good for those who love God, who are called according to his purpose. For those he foreknew he also predestined to be conformed to the image of his Son. . . . What then shall we say to this? If God is for us, who can be against us?
>
> Romans 8:28–29, 31 NABRE

When we try to dig ourselves out of a crushing defeat and find no rock bottom, only an endless labyrinth of tunnels where the anguish seems unending, we desperately need to know that God makes all things work for good. These words may sound like hollow promises when we are trying to move forward after betrayal by someone close to us. This is particularly true when family or friends are affected—for instance, if you're watching a spouse or one of your kids struggle with something really hard.

Although your tears matter and your hurt is real, this pain will not take over your whole life. How you've been mistreated isn't the most important aspect of your identity as you go forward. The Lord has called you for a purpose. He has chosen you to become like Jesus, his Son. Since God is *for* you, you can trust that, in the waiting and the weeping, he is creating an outcome for you that comes only from his heart for you.

Heavenly Father, I trust you with all the outcomes I'm praying for. I know you have my good at heart.

18

The Lord Will Never Leave Me

> Try to join me soon, for Demas, enamored of the present world, deserted me and went to Thessalonica, Crescens to Galatia, and Titus to Dalmatia. Luke is the only one with me. . . . Alexander the coppersmith did me a great deal of harm. . . . At my first defense no one appeared on my behalf, but everyone deserted me. . . . But the Lord stood by me and gave me strength.
>
> 2 Timothy 4:9–11, 14, 16–17 NABRE

Underneath the updates about his co-workers that Paul is giving his disciple Timothy, it is clear that he feels lonely. He's forsaken by Demas. The old team members Crescens and Titus now work in other places. Only Luke is left. Not only that—he has sustained injury and harm through Alexander's actions. And finally, when he really needed support, nobody showed up. Nobody.

In life and relationships, there are changes. People move on. People no longer want to share our vision. People don't have the courage to endure hard things. People whom we trusted with our heart turn on us. The weight of life that saddles each person with unexpected responsibility feels like too much. The fabric of relationships is torn.

Paul reaches out to a friend: "Try to join me soon," and proclaims: "The Lord stood by me." When you feel betrayed and left behind, these are two important things to remember. You can always reach out to someone who understands, and the Lord will never leave you.

Lord, show me the next steps. Keep me walking forward!

19

Jesus, Show Me the Next Step

> Let your speech always be gracious, seasoned with salt, so that you may know how you ought to answer everyone.
>
> Colossians 4:6

At some point, as you weather the storms of disappointment in your life, you may wonder whether you should have an honest conversation with the one who broke your heart or just walk away. Questions like the following will be important to ask yourself and pray about: Do I have enough clarity about what happened? Am I still too emotionally raw? How big a risk would such a conversation be? Is there any hope that it would have a positive outcome? What boundaries need to be put in place? What would indicate that it's time to say good-bye? How important is this relationship to me?

When you've been deeply affected by dysfunction, distress, and distrust within a personal or working relationship, it could take a long time to answer these questions for yourself. A frank and gracious conversation that honors the other person as well as yourself could clear the air in a friendship you value. What seemed like a betrayal may have been thoughtlessness, a mistake, or a decision made under duress. But you may need to wait or walk away from a difficult relationship that has become unsustainable. Whatever choice you make, God's Word invites you to use speech that is helpful, valuable, and wise.

Jesus, I'm not sure how to address the person who has so deeply hurt me. Guide me, teach me, mold me, help me. Amen.

20

I Am Ready, O God

Do not remember the former things,
    or consider the things of old.
I am about to do a new thing;
    now it springs forth, do you not perceive it?

Isaiah 43:18–19

It's scary to pick up the broken parts of one's story and move on. It's a risk to invest in yourself and a new future. You might wonder what will happen if you let go of painful memories and acknowledge that abundant life has begun to blossom around the very wounds that have so scarred your heart.

What are you willing to risk to discover the new thing God is doing in you?

God has been growing new life and purpose in your story. No matter how difficult things have been, you will discover that each struggling step has been a teacher. Even if every step forward has been followed by two steps back, you will never have reached a dead-end, but merely a turn in the road. Take a rest if you must, and then find new ways to engage life. Read. Reflect. Experience the world. Talk to others. Any glimmer of hope you feel will remind you that your life is not over. Notice how God is rebuilding your life and collaborate. Try new things. Allow your emotions to come and go. Grow inwardly strong.

I am ready, O God, I am ready. Do a new thing in me.

21

Jesus, You Help Me Move On

> [Mary Magdalene] stood weeping outside the tomb. . . . Jesus said to her, "Mary!" She turned and said to him in Hebrew, "Rabbouni!" (which means Teacher). . . . Mary Magdalene went and announced to the disciples, "I have seen the Lord."
>
> John 20:11, 16, 18

On the day after the Sabbath, Mary Magdalene returned to the tomb where Jesus had been laid, the place of her sorrow. She may have sought to find Jesus in her memory and feelings as she came to contemplate what she had lost. But Jesus did not appear to her there. Instead, it was only after she turned away from the tomb that she saw him standing before her. In your inspired imagination, consider her astonishment at seeing Jesus there, alive and radiant with glory. What did Mary experience when she once again heard her name on the lips of one she loved?

Maybe you, too, are still picking up memories and leafing through chapters of your life that are over forever. You might remember the real bonds of friendship you had with someone special. Maybe you thought you'd always have each other's backs, but it turned out that the other was heading a different way all along. You found your heart nailed to a cross of disappointment and rejection.

Like Mary, you need to "turn away from the tomb" and look for Jesus, who is gently sending you into a future he has prepared for you.

Praise be to you, Father, who have given us new birth into a living hope through the resurrection of Jesus Christ from the dead! (see 1 Peter 1:3)

22

Jesus, You Have Changed the Course of My Life

"I have compassion for the crowd, because they have been with me now for three days and have nothing to eat; and I do not want to send them away hungry, for they might faint on the way." . . . [He] took the seven loaves and the fish; and after giving thanks he broke them and gave them to the disciples, and the disciples gave them to the crowds. And all of them ate and were filled.

Matthew 15:32, 36–37

I can imagine Jesus looking out over the thousands of people sitting around him. Certainly, he read on each face their heart's response: joy, uncertainty, disbelief, or the inner debate of whether to hope this one last time. . . . Jesus had compassion on every single person, each of whom had a story, a sorrow, and a dream.

Jesus fed them, and they were filled. As he provided for the next few steps of their journey, they realized how much love they had received in their moment of need.

For you, too, Jesus provides these in-the-moment surprises of grace. Some may seem ordinary, yet as they accumulate they change the course of life. They may come in various forms: an insight, a book, a friend, a song, a different job, a group, a grace at prayer, the Eucharist. Just as Jesus concerned himself about the needs of the crowd, he gives you the same attention, as if you were the only person in the world.

Jesus, today I want to thank you for the many in-the-moment miracles you are giving to me. Open my eyes that I may see you always.

23

Lord, I Desire Everything You Wish for Me Now

Happy are those
    who do not follow the advice of the wicked . . .
but their delight is in the law of the LORD. . . .
They are like trees
    planted by streams of water,
which yield their fruit in its season,
    and their leaves do not wither.

PSALM 1:1–3

To be happy means "to delight in the Lord." I don't want to diminish the suffering of a soul jaded by loss. I want to say simply that new life will begin to emerge all around you when you choose to desire everything God wishes for you *now*—when you plant yourself, so to speak, near streams of living water, making decisions that will bear fruit in due time, and nourish yourself on what will make you flourish.

So commit yourself to your own joy. By letting grievances go, whenever and however you are able, you affirm that you are no longer held hostage by another. You affirm that the Lord himself is watching over you and revealing your way into the future.

Jesus, help me to relinquish what can't be regained, to recover what can still bless my life, and to replace what has not been helpful with what is wholesome and true. Amen.

24

Jesus, Help Me to Love Bravely

"I give you a new commandment: love one another. As I have loved you, so you also should love one another. This is how all will know that you are my disciples, if you have love for one another."

John 13:34–35 NABRE

Jesus pronounced these words just after one of his closest friends had left to betray him. Our life is full of all kinds of betrayals. Most of us have our "Judas." Jesus knows what it is to have your heart walked on after you've cared about and trusted someone. He knows the heart can harden, right where the hurt cuts most deeply.

Jesus invites us to keep our hearts soft. On the night when he stared into the darkness and knew that his death was approaching, he ate a last supper with even his betrayer. On the night when Jesus was abandoned by all, he continued to walk his Father's path. He kept in view the larger picture of redemption; he remembered you and me.

Keeping your heart soft is a beautiful witness to the world. You can begin by addressing the person or situation in whatever way makes sense, perhaps saying: "I know what you did. It hurt. It wounded me. It gave me scars that I may bear for the rest of my life. But I've chosen not to hold it against you." Whether you say these words directly, write them, or pray them in your heart, they are powerful words that witness love to the world.

Jesus, help me love bravely. Keep my heart soft.

25

Open My Heart to Love Again

> God's love was revealed among us in this way: God sent his only Son into the world so that we might live through him. . . . Beloved, since God loved us so much, we also ought to love one another.
>
> 1 John 4:9, 11

God's love is an invitation to live no longer out of what "they did to me," but out of what "God has done for me." That still might be hard to hear. Your heart may still shout, "It's not fair!" And it's the truth: whatever happened to you wasn't fair and should never have happened.

When I find my heart full of pain at the injustice that another has done to me, sometimes I picture Jesus between me and the person or group who betrayed me. I watch how Jesus looks at me. His gaze communicates tender sorrow for what I've endured and assurance that he will sustain me. I also watch how Jesus looks at the other person(s). Most often his gaze restores gentleness to me, allowing a sigh of relief to escape me as my heart gives up its weapons and accepts the way that Jesus loves us both.

To love is to take steps—even tiny ones—to move from resistance and unconcern to mercy, and to a tender hope that the source of our hurt will find the God who loves them. It is love that shifts the dynamic of the trauma.

Jesus, help me to believe in love, to open my heart to love again and to share that love with others.

26

I Renounce the Lies I Have Believed

You are my God; be gracious to me, Lord;
    to you I call all the day.
Gladden the soul of your servant;
    to you, Lord, I lift up my soul.
Lord, you are good and forgiving,
    most merciful to all who call on you.
LORD, hear my prayer;
    listen to my cry for help.

PSALM 86:2–6 NABRE

Set aside some quiet time alone. Pray the passage from Psalm 86 as a prayer and a plea. In your memory gently lift up the betrayal that has broken your heart. As you picture the event, ask Jesus, "Where were you at that moment?" Or "Where are you in this room right now?"

Wait for some insight, an image or word, or an *aha* moment. Freeze-frame that experience and soak in whatever Jesus helps you to see. What arises in your heart to say to him?

As you rest in what Jesus shows you, he may lead you to renounce the lies that the betrayal led you to believe about yourself and God, such as: I'm no good. God doesn't care. I don't belong. God doesn't love me. I'm powerless, worthless, unlovable. There's no future for me. I'll never get myself together.

Jesus may invite you to bury such judgments by proclaiming the truth about his love and fidelity: "Lord, you are good and forgiving *to me*. You are most merciful *to me* when I call on you." "O God, I believe that you are good, that you care about me, that you love me."

You, O Lord, are my God. Because of you I am good, worthy, and lovable.

27

Lord, You Are Making All Things New

> So if anyone is in Christ, there is a new creation: everything old has passed away; see, everything has become new!
>
> 2 Corinthians 5:17

It is by God's sheer grace that through Baptism each of us has been incorporated into Christ and made a child of God! Pause and read this simple sentence one more time. The sheer magnitude of God's outreach to each of us can take our breath away and make us cry out: It's amazing to be a Christian!

What happened when we were baptized is not a metaphor or a nice idea. It was utterly real. In and with Christ we have risen from the dead. We have been united to the Resurrected Christ. Actually, truly, we have been brought into a new and paschal way of living.

As we begin to experience the flashes of hope that healing brings, a deep reality opens up for us—we are made new because the infinite God personally loves us, with our whole story, every twist and turn of it. The choices now before us will become opportunities to live more fully because we know that we are loved.

As you continue to sort out what God wants for you in the future, you can adopt an always more Christ-like way of living. It's time to nurture a growing sense of peace, the restfulness of serenity and gratitude, the expanding horizon of hopefulness.

Lord, you make all things new!

28

You Show Me a Better Way

"Blessed are the merciful,
for they will be shown mercy."

MATTHEW 5:7 NABRE

Showing mercy is not easy. It is a strong virtue. It may take time for our hearts to be ready for this kind of love to take root in them. Mercy is not leniency or tolerance of injustice. Mercy demands that we be truthful with ourselves and with others. It is fed by an inward fountain of joy so that we act and speak without exploiting, retaliating, or manipulating others, but rather seeking their ultimate good and our own.

The Beatitudes tell us that, regardless of the circumstances, we can trust God to show his favor to us when we live their upside-down, counter-intuitive values. Like showing mercy. Like being pure in heart. Like being a peacemaker.

Our aches, hurts, and longings could leave us stewing in resentment. Through the lens of the Beatitudes, however, we remember that Jesus shows us a better way. We can ask ourselves: "What would this look like in a world where mercy was flowing in every direction?"

God has blessed the life you have. He accompanies you to the very edge of your hope. There, right there, he shows you mercy. The crisis you have weathered, through God's mercy, has become part of a divine story. You can say, "I am blessed."

Jesus, help me see new ways forward as I re-imagine what my situation would look like if mercy were flowing everywhere.

29

I'm Beginning to See That You Are Faithful

> Surely God is my salvation;
> I will trust, and will not be afraid,
> for the LORD GOD is my strength and my might;
> he has become my salvation. . . .
> Shout aloud and sing for joy, O royal Zion,
> for great in your midst is the Holy One of Israel.
>
> ISAIAH 12:2, 6

This passage from the prophet Isaiah has always captured my heart. In the past, in moments of deep sorrow and betrayal, I could barely utter the words. But now my heart sings them, even through tears.

It wasn't God's will for someone to betray you or treat you unjustly, but God does take what you have suffered and remake it so that it brings about your good. Only he can do this. Only God can take something that another meant for your harm and transform it so as to transform *you*—make you greater than you ever thought possible. It may take years, even decades, to realize that God has let nothing prevent him from accomplishing all he desires for you in his love, but one day you will know this. I promise. God will let nothing get in his way.

Lord, I'm beginning to see that you are faithful. I trust you to love me.

30

How Can I Thank You?

> Then I saw a new heaven and a new earth; for the first heaven and the first earth had passed away, and the sea was no more. And I saw the holy city, the new Jerusalem, coming down out of heaven from God, prepared as a bride adorned for her husband. And I heard a loud voice from the throne saying,
>
> "See, the home of God is among mortals.
> He will dwell with them . . .
> he will wipe every tear from their eyes." . . .
>
> And the one who was seated on the throne said, "See, I am making all things new."
>
> Revelation 21:1–5

Perhaps as you began this journey, you felt deeply wounded from another's betrayal. As you have prayed, it is God himself who has brought about something new within you. Now would be a good time to ask the Lord: What is it that you want me to know?

Take a moment and allow an image or word that encapsulates your experience to form in your mind. When you remember this symbol, you will be able to recapture some of the gifts God has given you as well as the most essential reflections you have incorporated into your healing journey.

Ask Jesus for a core image of how he sees you when he looks at you now. You can do this every day because each morning is a new beginning and each evening witnesses the many subtle and not so subtle transformations that mark the beauty of a life that God is continuing to make new.

How can I thank you, Jesus, for the graces that have washed, healed, strengthened, and renewed me?

Prayers

Psalm 18

I love you, Lord, my strength,
    Lord, my rock, my fortress, my deliverer,
My God, my rock of refuge,
    my shield, my saving horn, my stronghold!
Praised be the Lord, I exclaim!
    I have been delivered from my enemies.
The cords of death encompassed me;
    the torrents of destruction terrified me.
The cords of Sheol encircled me;
    the snares of death lay in wait for me.
In my distress I called out: Lord!
    I cried out to my God.
From his temple he heard my voice;
    my cry to him reached his ears.
The earth rocked and shook;
    the foundations of the mountains trembled;
    they shook as his wrath flared up.
Smoke rose from his nostrils,
    a devouring fire from his mouth;

it kindled coals into flame.
He parted the heavens and came down,
a dark cloud under his feet.
Mounted on a cherub he flew,
borne along on the wings of the wind.
He made darkness his cloak around him;
his canopy, water-darkened storm-clouds.
From the gleam before him, his clouds passed,
hail and coals of fire.
The LORD thundered from heaven;
the Most High made his voice resound.
He let fly his arrows and scattered them;
shot his lightning bolts and dispersed them.
Then the bed of the sea appeared;
the world's foundations lay bare,
At your rebuke, O LORD,
at the storming breath of your nostrils.
He reached down from on high and seized me;
drew me out of the deep waters.
He rescued me from my mighty enemy,
from foes too powerful for me.
They attacked me on my day of distress,
but the LORD was my support.
He set me free in the open;
he rescued me because he loves me.

PSALM 18:2–20 NABRE

Enter My Life

Open, O doors and bolts of my heart, that Christ
the King of Glory may enter!
Enter, O my Light, and enlighten my darkness;
Enter, O my Life, and resurrect my deadness;
Enter, O my Physician, and heal my wounds;
Enter, O Divine Fire, and burn up the thorns of my
sins;
Ignite my inward parts and my heart with the
flame of Thy love.
Enter, O my King, and destroy in me the kingdom
of sin;
Sit on the throne of my heart and reign in me
alone, O my King and Lord.

DIMITRY OF ROSTOCV (1651–1709),
CANONIZED A SAINT IN THE RUSSIAN ORTHODOX CHURCH

A Prayer to Believe in Love

So many sorrows. So many tears. Such loss. A tidal
wave of pain. I thought I couldn't go on. I felt
it was the end . . .
It wasn't.
Your love, O Lord, is mightier than all.

Before I could love you, you chose to love me.
Before the mountains were born and the earth was brought forth, you loved me.
Before the foundation of the world, you had me in mind.
You already knew me. You already loved me.
You knit me together in my mother's womb.
You are always with me. You know everything about me.
You know more about me than I know about myself.
You know what is possible because you have always loved me, and your dream for me still stands.
Your love will be with me always.
Nothing can separate me from your love. No one can take me from your presence. No sorrow can blot out the light of your goodness.
Your loving me never ceases. Your mercies never come to an end. Every morning you are there without fail, with your compassion that makes life possible.
You, O Lord, are love itself. Help me never to doubt that you see me, that you hear me, that

you know every detail of my life, and that you believe in me.

Help me, Lord, to believe in love once again.

Based on Psalm 90, Psalm 139, Lamentations 3, and Romans 8

Kathryn J. Hermes, FSP

Heal Me, Lord

Heal me, Lord, that I may be healed;
save me, that I may be saved,
for you are my praise.

Jeremiah 17:14 NABRE

Sub Tuum Praesidium

This prayer, known in Latin as Sub Tuum Praesidium and first found in a Greek papyrus, c. 300 A.D., is the oldest known prayer to the Virgin.

We turn to you for protection,
Holy Mother of God.
Listen to our prayers
and help us in our needs.
Save us from every danger,
glorious and blessed Virgin.

Prayer for the Healing of Memories

Loving Father, I come before you with faith, trusting in your unconditional and constant love for me. Jesus has promised that whatever we ask for in his name we will receive, provided it be according to your holy will and for the good of my soul. I come to you believing in that promise.

I come as I am, in all my woundedness and visited by painful memories that still surface in my heart and mind and cause so much anguish and distress. You know how much I suffer because of these memories.

I beg you, enter my heart and heal all my wounded emotions. Bring your healing love into every corner of my being. Release all the buried negative memories and unhealed hurts that block the flow of your grace, robbing me of your peace, love, and joy. Help me to accept them as part of my salvation history and your redeeming love.

Remove every feeling of sadness, loneliness, fear, and anxiety. Wash away all guilt, despair, feelings of betrayal and rejection. Heal all feelings of anger, hatred, resentment, and bitterness.

Pour out your Spirit of healing on all the memories and emotions that cause feelings of hopelessness, discouragement, helplessness, shame, and despair. Grant me the grace to forgive all who have hurt me and likewise to be forgiven by those whom I have harmed. And then, dear Father, after I have been healed, make me a joyful witness of your healing power, that I may bring glory, honor, and praise to you.

I ask everything in Jesus' name. Amen.

Mary Leonora Wilson, FSP

Heart of Love

O Heart of love,
I place my trust entirely in you.
Though I fear all things from my weakness,
I hope all things from your goodness!

Saint Margaret Mary Alacoque

Thank You.

Your purchase of this book and engagement with our other projects supports us in the work we do as Daughters of St. Paul. This book is the fruit of our consecrated life, prayer, and mission of communicating God's love.

We hold you and all your intentions in our prayers. We invite you to connect with us or send us prayer intentions at pauline.org.